HAYAT SINDI

Brilliant Biochemist

Jill C. Wheeler

ABDO Publishing Company

visit us at
www.abdopublishing.com

Printed in the United States of America, North Mankato, Minnesota.
052012
092012

 PRINTED ON RECYCLED PAPER

Cover Photos: Jonathan Torgovnik/Reportage by Getty Images; Thinkstock
Interior Photos: Alamy p. 13; iStockphoto pp. 7, 17; Jonathan Torgovnik/Reportage by
    Getty Images p. 11; courtesy kthread / Kristen Taylor p. 21; courtesy PopTech pp. 5, 9, 15, 19,
    23, 25, 27

Series Coordinator: BreAnn Rumsch
Editors: Megan M. Gunderson, BreAnn Rumsch
Art Direction: Neil Klinepier

Library of Congress Cataloging-in-Publication Data

Wheeler, Jill C., 1964-
  Hayat Sindi : brilliant biochemist / Jill C. Wheeler.
    p. cm. -- (Women in science)
  Audience: 8-12
  Includes index.
  ISBN 978-1-61783-450-9
  1. Sindi, Hayat--Juvenile literature. 2. Women biochemists--Saudi Arabia--Biography--
Juvenile literature. 3. Biochemists--Saudi Arabia--Biography--Juvenile literature. I. Title.
  QP511.8.S556W44 2013
  572.092--dc23
  [B]
                          2012011516

CONTENTS

HAYAT SINDI

"For me, science is a universal language that transcends nationality, religion, and gender. It can help solve any problem our world faces."

— *Hayat Sindi*

Hayat Sindi is out to make a difference in the world. Her journey has brought her from Saudi Arabia to the United States. She has overcome many barriers to become one of the world's leading young scientists.

One of Sindi's scientific discoveries helps **cancer** patients get the right medicines. Another helps people **diagnose** illnesses even if they live miles away from a doctor's office. Sindi also developed a way to turn **sewage** water into drinking water!

Sindi believes science should benefit everyone. She thinks scientists can create affordable, simple solutions to many of the world's problems.

As an Arab, Sindi hopes to change science in the Middle East. She is especially interested in getting more Middle Eastern women to work in science.

As a young person, Sindi had a love of knowledge. She admired people who served others. Today, she is dedicated to the same goal.

TRADITIONAL HOME

>> *In Saudi Arabia, women must get permission from their husbands or fathers in order to take a job.*

In the early 1970s, Hayat Sulaiman Sindi was born into a traditional **Muslim** family. The Sindi family lived in Mecca, Saudi Arabia.

In Saudi Arabia, Islam governs many parts of life. Men and women are separated except when they are at home. Women are not allowed to drive cars. In public, most cover themselves with a long black cloak called an abaya. Many also wear a head scarf called a hijab.

Hayat is the oldest of eight children. She has five sisters and two brothers. Her father encouraged the children to read. Hayat especially loved *National Geographic* magazine.

By reading, Hayat learned about famous scientists and their work. People such as Marie Curie and Albert Einstein became her heroes. She also admired Muslim scientists. These included philosopher and physician Ibn Sina and mathematician al-Khwarizmi.

Muslims consider Mecca to be a holy city. They believe Mecca is where the prophet Muhammad was born.

FIB FOR A FUTURE

Hayat started school when she was six years old. She was an excellent student. By high school, she was performing at the top of her class.

After high school, Hayat was accepted into medical school. She began taking classes. However, opportunities for women in science were limited in Saudi Arabia. Hayat would have to leave home to achieve her dreams.

In Saudi **culture**, a woman living alone in another country is considered dishonorable. Hayat knew her decision to leave would be hard for her family. To make it easier on them, she told a lie. She said she had been accepted to a university in London, England.

Hayat's father did not want her to go. However, he wanted her to have a good education. Eventually, he realized there was little choice. He reluctantly agreed to let her go to England.

Hayat's family found out about her lie years later when she mentioned it during a speech.

DON'T LET ME DOWN

Hayat arrived in London in 1991. She did not speak a word of English. And since her acceptance had been a lie, she had no university to turn to.

Hayat spent her first night at a **youth hostel**. All alone in a strange city, she felt panicked. Hayat's father had given her a return plane ticket, just in case. She was tempted to use it.

But Hayat remembered what her father had told her before she left home. "Don't let me down," he had said. So Hayat did not use the ticket. She decided to be brave.

Hayat went to an Islamic **cultural** center. There, workers found her a **translator** to help her meet with college officials.

The officials realized Hayat did not understand the admission process. She thought colleges accepted any students who wanted to learn. But there was much more to do before continuing her education.

Sadly, Hayat's father died in 2010. But she knew how proud he had been of her. After his death, she found newspaper clippings about her work under his pillow.

LIFE IN LONDON

» *To learn English, Sindi watched British news and television programs.*

Sindi learned that to become a student she had to pass entrance examinations. And, she learned that her previous college classes would not count. She would have to start from scratch.

Sindi spent the next year preparing for school. She studied for hours on end. She also learned to speak English. All the while, she worried that she would fail and bring dishonor to her family. Yet after much hard work, Sindi passed the exams! She was accepted at King's College in central London.

In 1993, Sindi's hard work paid off. She received the college's Princess Ann Award for her work in the field of allergies. Two years later, she graduated.

King's College is one of the world's leading research universities.

DREAM COME TRUE

Sindi's next goal was to begin the research she had dreamed of. She wanted to study medicines and their chemical compounds. However, a machine for this task did not yet exist. So, Sindi switched her focus to **biotechnology**.

Next, Sindi applied for a grant at Cambridge University. She had to convince school officials that she could succeed. At the time, biotechnology was considered a field for men. Still, Sindi refused to give up. She became the first Arab woman to study biotechnology at Cambridge.

Meanwhile, Sindi also struggled to maintain her Arab identity. One Cambridge scientist advised her to stop wearing a hijab if she wanted to succeed. He even said she would fail in three months if she did not.

Sindi proved that scientist wrong. In 2001, she earned her **PhD** in biotechnology. She became the first woman to do so.

Cambridge officials appointed Sindi as a senior lecturer. She taught classes at the university's International School of Medicine.

While Sindi wears the traditional head scarf, she likes to pair it with fashionable high-heeled shoes or boots. She says scientists do not have to be geeks!

15

HUNTING FOR CANCER

For Sindi, **biotechnology** was a perfect fit. She likes to remind people that this science is as old as baking bread! As a modern science, it benefits people's lives in larger ways.

Sindi was still in her twenties when she made her first major scientific contribution. She invented a machine called the Magnetic Acoustic Resonance Sensor (MARS). It can detect the type of **cancer** a person has. Once this is known, doctors can give patients the right medicines. MARS can even **diagnose** cancer in its early stages.

For Sindi's next project, she focused on bacteria. She and her team used it to make **sewage** water clean enough to drink! Best of all, this could be done at a very low cost. Sindi's work helped poor communities that lacked proper plumbing and water treatment facilities.

Sindi invented and patented the MARS machine during her time at Cambridge. Cambridge is one of the world's oldest universities. It has operated for more than 800 years!

WORLD TRAVELER

>> *Sindi's hobbies include travel, horseback riding, poetry, music, painting, and interior design.*

As the first female **biotechnology** expert, Sindi became well known in the science community. She was asked to attend meetings around the world. And she received many awards in Saudi Arabia. Sindi even presented her work to the British House of Commons.

Sindi gave many television and radio interviews. She also spoke at an event at the University of California–Berkeley. Her speech inspired other women to follow careers in science. And in London, she spoke on the image of women in the Persian Gulf.

As Sindi's reputation grew, demand for her help increased. She worked on many biotechnology projects. She met with clients in North America, Europe, and the Middle East. She used her experience and imagination to help them solve problems. She focused on health care, oil, water, and the **environment**.

Today, Sindi often gives speeches that address science, women, and Arab life.

PEDALING FOR PEACE

Even with her heavy workload, Sindi found time to support her **culture**. In 2005, she joined about 250 other women from 25 different countries on a bicycle ride for peace.

Sindi represented Saudi Arabia in the ride. Her bicycle featured the green Saudi Arabian flag. She also wore a necklace with a picture of Saudi Arabia's King Abdullah.

The ride was called Follow the Women. It covered nearly 200 miles (320 km)! It began in Beirut, Lebanon, and wound through Syria and Jordan. It finished in Ramallah, Palestine.

In the Middle East, women do not often ride bicycles. So, this event caught the eyes of many people! This helped spread the message that Middle Eastern leaders needed to focus on peace between their nations. Ride organizers pointed out that violence in the Middle East often harms women and children the most.

Sindi has always been proud of her culture. However, she also understands the challenges within it.

HARVARD

In 2007, Sindi was invited to become a visiting scholar at Harvard University in Cambridge, Massachusetts. There, she worked with Professor George Whitesides. He worked to create products for developing countries. Sindi was the first **Muslim** scientist to join the effort.

The lab undertook many experiments in **biotechnology** and **chemistry**. Sindi's work focused on how these sciences could be used to better process and store oil.

Meanwhile, Sindi knew that millions of people around the world lacked access to modern health care technology. Any care they did receive often took place without electricity or clean water.

Sindi wanted to create a tool for **diagnosing** diseases more easily without the need for a lab. In 2007, she cofounded a company called Diagnostics for All. Scientists there aimed to develop a simple way to detect many diseases by testing saliva, urine, or blood.

Creating affordable health care solutions excites Sindi. Her focus is often on helping developing countries.

PAPER MAGIC

>> *Sindi and Dr. Whitesides went on to start a new company called Paper Diagnostics, Inc.*

By 2008, the Diagnostics for All team had invented their tool. It was a piece of paper! But it wasn't just regular, everyday paper. This paper was treated with special chemicals.

Each piece of paper is no bigger than a postage stamp. Due to the chemicals, it turns colors when it comes in contact with bodily fluids. Various colors indicate whether certain health conditions are present.

Sindi asked doctors in poor, rural areas what test would help them the most. She learned many medicines used to treat diseases such as **AIDS** can harm the liver. So, Sindi developed a test that can determine the health of a person's liver.

In 2008, Sindi's team won two major awards for their invention. They won the Massachusetts Institute of Technology's $100k Entrepreneurship Competition. They were the first **nonprofit** team ever to win! They also won Harvard's Business Plan Contest. This was the first time one team had ever captured both awards in the same year.

Diagnostics for All plans to someday be able to test for tuberculosis, malaria, HIV/AIDS, diabetes, and kidney disease.

PRACTICING PASSION

Sindi became the first Arab woman to be named a PopTech fellow in 2009. PopTech works to support scientific discovery.

Sindi enjoys talking about her work. She also encourages others to find their passion. She is especially interested in helping Middle Eastern women and girls believe in themselves. Sindi wants them to understand that they can transform society.

Sindi also wants to see **Muslim** countries focus more on science and technology. To this end, she launched a new foundation in 2011. It is called the Institute for Imagination and Ingenuity.

The foundation helps young Muslims who attend college outside their home countries. It helps them find money to develop their ideas. And, it encourages them to bring their ideas and abilities back to their homelands.

Albert Einstein once said that imagination is more important than knowledge. Sindi strongly agrees. So, her foundation aims to help people make a difference using both. Sindi's message is simple. She tells people to find a mission in life and contribute something to humanity.

For Hayat Sindi, science was the key. She believes that science and society go hand in hand. She also feels science should be used for the benefit of others, especially the developing world. Sindi is committed to using science to make the world a better place. She says, "Small people can achieve big dreams."

Today, only about 14% of Saudi Arabian workers are women. Sindi hopes she can help change that.

TIMELINE

EARLY 1970s

Hayat Sindi was born in Mecca, Saudi Arabia.

1991

Hayat arrived in London, England, where she learned to speak English.

1995

Sindi earned her bachelor's degree from King's College in London.

2001

Sindi became the first woman to earn a PhD in biotechnology from Cambridge University.

2005

Sindi took part in the Follow the Women bicycle ride.

2007

Sindi became a visiting scholar at Harvard University. She was the first Muslim scientist to join Professor George Whitesides's laboratory.

2008

With her team from Diagnostics for All, Sindi won two major awards for the invention of a paper diagnostic tool.

2011

Sindi launched her Institute for Imagination and Ingenuity.

DIG DEEPER

Dr. Hayat Sindi knows that the world is full of substances. Scientists learn about them by testing their properties. Litmus paper is a simple way to measure the property of pH, or the level of acids and bases. Make your own litmus paper to learn more about the substances in your home.

SUPPLIES:
• 4 white index cards • red cabbage • water • a large pot • a glass dish • a knife • a stove • scissors

INSTRUCTIONS: *Always ask an adult for help!*

1 Have an adult help you with all of step 1. Slice up the cabbage. Put the slices in the pot and fill with water until the slices are covered. Boil, with no lid, for 30 minutes. Carefully pour the cabbage juice into a low glass dish. Do not add more water to the juice.

2 Soak the index cards in the cabbage juice for about 20 to 30 minutes. Remove the cards and let them dry. They should be light purple.

3 Use scissors to cut the dry cards into 1-inch (2.5 cm) strips. The strips can be stored in a plastic bag. Throw out the remaining cabbage juice.

4 Now you are ready to test pH! Start with lemon juice. Then try tap water. Make a solution of 2 tablespoons (30 mL) of water and 1 teaspoon (5 mL) of baking soda to try next. Use a different strip for each substance. Does each strip turn a different color?

Think of some other substances to test at home, such as vinegar, Coca-Cola, and milk. Which ones turn the strips green? These are bases. Which ones turn the strips pink? These are acids. Do any strips turn blue? What do you think that means?

GLOSSARY

AIDS – acquired immunodeficiency syndrome. A disease that weakens the immune system. It is caused by the human immunodeficiency virus (HIV).

biotechnology – a science that studies ways to use living things such as cells and bacteria to make useful products, such as medicine.

cancer – any of a group of often deadly diseases marked by harmful changes in the normal growth of cells. Cancer can spread and destroy healthy tissues and organs.

chemistry – a science that studies substances and the changes that they go through.

culture – the customs, arts, and tools of a nation or a people at a certain time. Something related to culture is cultural.

diagnose – to recognize something, such as a disease, by signs, symptoms, or tests.

environment – all the surroundings that affect the growth and well-being of a living thing.

Muslim – a person who follows Islam. Islam is a religion based on the teachings of the prophet Muhammad as they appear in the Koran.

nonprofit – not existing or carried on for the purpose of making a profit.

PhD – doctor of philosophy. Usually, this is the highest degree a student can earn.

sewage – waste materials carried off by sewers.

translator – a person who changes words from one language into another.

youth hostel – a supervised lodging for young travelers.

WEB SITES

To learn more about Hayat Sindi, visit ABDO Publishing Company online. Web sites about Hayat Sindi are featured on our Book Links page. These links are routinely monitored and updated to provide the most current information available.
www.abdopublishing.com

INDEX